BETWEEN TWO WORLDS

A Creative Minds Biography

BETWEEN TWO WORLDS

A Story about Pearl Buck

by Barbara Mitchell

illustrations by Karen Ritz

M Millbrook Press/Minneapolis

For Martie Snover

Millbrook Press, Inc.
A division of Lerner Publishing Group
241 First Avenue North
Minneapolis, MN 55401 U.S.A.

Website address: www.lernerbooks.com

Library of Congress Cataloging-in-Publication Data

Mitchell, Barbara, 1941–
    Between two worlds: a story about Pearl Buck / by Barbara Mitchell,
illustrations by Karen Ritz.
        p.   cm. — (A creative minds book)
    Summary: A biography of the woman who was awarded both the
Pulitzer and Nobel prizes for literature.
    ISBN-13: 978–0–87614–332–2 (lib. bdg. : alk. paper)
    ISBN-10: 0–87614–332–X (lib. bdg. : alk. paper)
    1. Buck, Pearl S. (Pearl Sydenstricker), 1892–1973—Biography—
Juvenile literature. 2. Novelists, American—20th century—
Biography—Juvenile literature. 3. China—Social life and customs—
Juvenile literature. [1. Buck, Pearl S. (Pearl Sydenstricker),
1892–1973. 2. Authors, American. 3. China—Social life and
customs.] I. Ritz, Karen, ill. II. Title. III. Series.
PS3503.U198Z72 1988
813'.52—dc19 [92]   88–6095

Manufactured in the United States of America
6 7 8 9 10 11 – JR – 11 10 09 08 07 06

Table of Contents

Chapter One

"Little foreign devil!"

The cruel name followed Pearl Sydenstricker down the crowded Chinkiang street. It rang in her ears as she went out the gate to the ancient walled city. It was with her in the valley bright with Chinese cabbages and on the climb to her home high in the jade green hills.

It was true that Pearl was a foreigner. Her American missionary parents had brought Pearl to China not long after her birth in 1892. But Pearl was no devil. Of that she was sure. "If those children knew me, they would not call me a devil," she told Wang Amah.

"It is only that your yellow hair and blue eyes are so strange to them," Wang Amah said. She handed Pearl a bowl of cabbage and fresh white bean curd.

Pearl's parents would be sitting down to their American-style lunch now, but Pearl much preferred to eat with Wang Amah. Pearl thought Chinese food was the most wonderful food in the world, even better than the snowy coconut cakes her mother baked.

They ate in Wang Amah's neat little room. Pearl pulled a bamboo stool up close to the woman who had been her nurse for most of her eight years. "Tell me about the river dragon," she said.

The room filled with the gentle singsong of Wang Amah's storytelling.

"Now tell about when you were very young," Pearl demanded.

Wang Amah was old. Her face was brown and lined like a walnut. She had only six teeth. She knew more stories than anyone else in the world, Pearl thought.

Pearl loved stories. She could not get enough of them. If Wang Amah were busy, Pearl would go to the cook for a story. If the cook were busy, Pearl would go to the ginger jar where she kept her pocket money. Coins jingling in her pocket, she would run barefoot through the tall pampas grass in search of the wandering storyteller.

Sometimes she found the magical man in the village square. Sometimes the tinkle of his brass bells brought her to a farmer's field. When his tales were told, the storyteller was always given a bowl of tea. When the tea was gone, the storyteller would pass the bowl to his listeners. Pearl would drop her coins in with the rest. The storyteller must be paid.

The pocket money that Pearl so often used to pay the storyteller came from stories written by Pearl herself. Pearl had written her first story when she was only six. In a letter to the editor of the Christian Observer, a newspaper from Louisville, Kentucky, she had told about the recent death of her brother. Four-year-old Clyde was in heaven now, she had explained, along with another brother, Artie, and her two sisters, Maudie and Edith. Artie and the two little sisters had all died before she was born. Now, she had written, there was only her brother Edgar, away at college in America, and Pearl herself.

Seeing her own words in print was thrilling. Pearl had written another story and sent it to a contest for children offered by the *Shanghai Mercury*. That story was followed by another, and another. The editor of the English newspaper printed in Shanghai paid for the prizewinning stories and was keeping Pearl's coin jar full.

On rainy days, Pearl went to her father's library. High on a top shelf was a set of beautiful blue books. They were written by an Englishman named Charles Dickens. Pearl's missionary father did not approve of the novels being in the house. Fiction was worldly and a waste of time, Absalom Sydenstricker said. The books belonged to Pearl's mother, Carie. Reading novels was one of Carie's secret joys. Dickens's droll characters made her smile.

Like her mother, Pearl loved the people in Mr. Dickens's books. The fictional people in Dickens's novels were as real as life to Pearl. She made up her mind that someday she would be a novelist.

People were what Pearl loved best besides stories. As often as possible, she ran down to the pond where the Chinese farmers' wives did their laundry. She and the farm children would play.

Often she would also sit and talk with their mothers.

"The mothers were not very friendly to me today," Pearl reported at supper one night in the spring of 1900.

Carie looked at her husband. There was trouble in China. England, many European countries, and Russia were each claiming a part of China as their own. The foreign colony builders were seizing control of the rivers and building railroads to carry Chinese products out of China. Empress Tzu Hsi had turned against foreigners, it was said. She wanted China rid of them and their Western ideas.

"Your friends are frightened," Pearl's mother said. "Great changes are taking place in their lives."

"The Chinese and their empress are concerned," Absalom explained. "Their land is being divided up between foreign countries, and they have no army to protect it."

Only a few days later, Pearl came home from school with more upsetting news. "Nobody would sit with me today," she said. "Why?"

"It is because you are white," her mother said.

"But I haven't done anything!" Pearl exclaimed.

Her mother nodded. "I know, Pearl."

"Is it because I am American?" Pearl asked.

Her mother shook her head. "It is because in their fear, your schoolmates are lumping all white people together," she said.

"We must sympathize with the Chinese," Pearl's father said. The United States had no plan to build a colony in China, but he was saddened that his country was doing nothing to help the Chinese keep their country from being divided. "Some Chinese soldiers called the Boxers have banded together, trying to help the empress," he went on. "They are burning houses where white people and people with Western ideas live. The United States Consul has sent out a notice. We must be prepared to leave at any time."

Pearl could not believe it. She felt like a stranger in the country she thought of as home.

"How will we know when to go?" she asked.

"When the Consul sends up a red flag, it will be time," Carie said quietly. She was frightened for Pearl and for Pearl's new baby sister, Grace. She did not tell Pearl that the children of a missionary in a nearby town had already been killed by the Boxers.

Carie planned a secret escape route. They would

go through the thick bamboos in the backyard, on through the reeds that grew by the ponds in the valley, and straight to the dock in Chinkiang. An American ship would be waiting to carry them south to Shanghai. The port at Shanghai was the exit to the Western world. If need be, they could sail for America.

The red flag went up at noon on a humid August day. Pearl sadly went out to the backyard and said good-bye to her pheasants and her rabbit. "You will remember to feed Neb, won't you?" she said to her father. Nebuchadnezzar was an old gray dog Pearl had adopted.

"Yes, Pearl," her father said. Absalom Sydenstricker would not be going with his family. He felt it his place to stand by the Chinese Christians.

It was Wang Amah who led the way through the bamboos. Next came Pearl, carrying a few of her best-loved books. Her mother followed with Grace. Then came her father with a small bundle of food and clothing for them all. The silent procession made its way through the back streets of Chinkiang.

A ship was waiting in the caramel-colored Yangtze River, just as the Consul had said. Wang Amah went aboard the ship, followed by Pearl and then Carie, holding Grace. Pearl stood on deck, waving good-bye to her father until she could no longer see him. She watched until the coolies running about the docks with heavy loads of rice and tea became only spots in the distance.

Chapter Two

A year went by before the Boxer Rebellion was quieted and Absalom Sydenstricker was able to bring his family back from Shanghai. Pearl had many things to tell him. Their tiny apartment had been hot and stuffy. Grace had cried a lot. Wang Amah had taken them for walks to a little park by the water. "And we saw a steamship from America!" she finished.

Her father had his own news to share. The mission board had granted him leave. They would all be going to America for a year.

"Think of it, Pearl," her mother said. "We are going *home*." Home to Carie was the big white house at the foot of the Allegheny Mountains in Hillsboro, West Virginia.

Pearl was full of questions about the land of her birth. Would there be children there for her to play with? Where would she stay? Would she go to school? There would be ample time for questions. The journey by steamship would cover over six thousand miles and take a month.

When at last their ship docked in San Francisco, Pearl and Grace stared wide-eyed at the tall buildings. They looked with wonder at the magic of running water in their hotel and at the gaslights that turned the city into a fairyland at night. San Francisco was just the beginning of their journey. There was still the train ride that would take them across the United States to West Virginia.

Pearl spent happy days picnicking, picking grapes, and milking the cow at her grandfather's house in Hillsboro. She went to third grade in an American school. It was neither the beautiful West Virginia mountains nor the school that impressed her most, though. What Pearl liked best were the people. Pearl got to know her older brother Edgar, and she discovered that she had aunts and uncles and cousins to call her own. There were children who looked like her!

When winter came, Pearl spent many cold evenings in front of her grandfather's big fireplace.

Curled up beside him, she told her grandfather all about Wang Amah and their cook and the farm families down by the pond. "If only you could know them, you would love them, too," she said.

At the end of the school year, the Sydenstrickers returned to China. Pearl was only 10, but she had made a discovery that would influence her entire life. She belonged to two worlds. America had given her her identity, but China had nurtured her. Pearl felt as though she had a foot in each world, and she did not know how to bring her two worlds together.

Pearl spent her mornings studying with her mother now. It was time for her to learn the American history and literature that she could not get in a Chinese school. Pearl learned quickly and had a lot of time to herself once the lessons were done. She spent her free hours wandering up and down the streets of Chinkiang. A change had taken place in Chinkiang in the year that she had been away. She saw an even greater fear in the eyes of the Chinese. To gain control over the Boxer Rebellion, foreign powers had sent British, Russian, German, French, Austrian, Italian, Japanese, and American soldiers into China. The Chinese had suffered greatly.

Every afternoon at 2:00, Pearl had a lesson with Mr. Kung. Teacher Kung unwrapped the square of black silk that held his treasure of books and taught Pearl to read and write in Chinese. Pearl told him all about America. "We had milk—from a cow!" she said. In China, what little milk there was came from water buffalo.

"And I have a grandfather!" Pearl said, "Old and very kind—like you."

Teacher Kung listened politely. Deep down, he wondered if a white person could be kind. During the rebellion, his fine old house had been destroyed by German soldiers.

An alarming thought took hold of Pearl. "Did American soldiers hurt people in China?" she asked.

Her teacher slowly nodded his head. It was so.

Pearl was deeply distressed. People of her kind had done terrible things in China. "But that was not my grandfather," she said. "Oh, Teacher Kung, if only you could know him, the two of you could talk, and you would understand him."

At that, Pearl put her head down on the oval dining room table and began to sob. She knew there was little chance that the teacher she loved and the grandfather she loved would ever meet.

Chapter Three

The year Pearl was 15, there was a great famine in China. For months, there was no rain. The farmers could not grow enough food to feed their own families, let alone to sell. Starving families poured into the cities, hoping to find something to eat.

There was no snowy coconut cake for Christmas dinner that year. The Sydenstrickers took the money they would have spent on a Christmas feast and bought rice to feed the hungry people.

Carie cooked huge pots of the rice. Pearl and seven-year-old Grace spent the day handing bowl after bowl of rice through the city gate to the families camped along the Chinkiang wall. The famine lasted until spring.

The experience made a deep impression on Pearl. She could not forget the thin little hands that had reached out to her for survival. She sat by the hour brooding over the sad fate of the Chinese farmers.

"You never play your piano anymore," Carie remarked. Pearl shrugged her shoulders. Her music no longer brought her joy. Carie and Absalom were worried. Their 16-year-old daughter needed some American friends her own age, they felt. They decided to send her to the Jewell School in Shanghai where she would meet other American girls, daughters of missionaries and businessmen.

A Chinese tailor was called in. Carie brought out her American magazines, and the tailor faithfully recreated the designs, trimming the fine Chinese silk and linen with his exquisite embroidery. Pearl arrived at Miss Jewell's in style.

The Jewell School required its students to teach sewing to Chinese servant girls who lived in the city. When the young Chinese girls found that

Pearl understood their language, they poured out the stories of their lives to her. Pearl got so caught up in the stories she was hearing that she spent almost no time at all with her classmates. "You needn't become involved," Miss Jewell said.

But Pearl wanted to be involved. And furthermore, she said, she did not believe in forcing the Chinese to adopt Western ways and religion.

By 1910, Pearl was ready for college. Her brother Edgar was married now and lived in Lynchburg, Virginia. It was decided that Pearl would attend Randolph-Macon Woman's College there. Carie got down the trunks and started packing. The whole family would accompany Pearl on this trip to Virginia.

The night before they were to sail, Pearl lay in bed listening to the deep toll of the bell in the Buddhist temple down the hill. How she loved that sound! Would she ever return to China? She lay awake, wondering.

On her first day of college, Pearl stood silent and alone. The chattering American girls that filled the dining room all seemed to know one another. Pearl looked down at her linen dress made so lovingly by a Chinese tailor. The length was wrong. The long, slender sleeves were wrong.

All the American girls wore "puffs" for sleeves. She looked at the other girls' hair. They all had fake curls pinned to their heads. Pearl's braid tied at the back of her neck looked out of place. Carie's fashion magazines had been out of date. It seemed hours before a country girl, looking almost as plain as Pearl herself, asked Pearl to sit with her.

Being ignored would not be Pearl's problem, she found. She soon became the object of conversation. In the dormitory, the classroom, and the dining room, the girls gathered in tight little groups and, staring in her direction, broke into hushed conversation. "She's so odd . . . those Chinese dresses . . . the shoes." Pearl could not help but overhear.

Why don't they ever ask me about China? she wondered. All the girls ever talked about were boys and football and their sororities.

One got into the all-important sororities by invitation, Pearl learned. She was not invited. Pearl Sydenstricker did not belong, and she wanted desperately to do so. With money earned from tutoring, she bought herself dresses from the most fashionable store in town. She replaced the hand-crafted shoes made by her Chinese cobbler with store-bought shoes. She put up her hair. Pearl was invited to join a sorority. Outwardly, she was accepted as an American. Inwardly, Pearl knew there was something terribly wrong. A part of her would always be Chinese. She could not simply throw away the world that had made her.

The years at Randolph-Macon showed Pearl to be an outstanding student. When a writing contest was announced for senior students, Pearl entered it with joy. She still wanted to be a writer. The contest offered awards for best story and best poem. Pearl won both.

After graduation, Pearl was invited to stay and teach psychology at the college. She was torn between a desire to see more of America and her homesickness for China. There would be greater teaching opportunities for her in America. She would stay.

Pearl had taught for just one semester when disturbing news arrived from China. Wang Amah had died. Carie was ill with a tropical disease. Pearl was badly needed at home, her father wrote. It was 1914, and the start of World War I made this a bad time to travel, but Pearl insisted. In November, she boarded a ship for China.

Chapter Four

Pearl now knew how she would bring her two worlds together. She would do it through her writing. She would be a novelist, just as she had always thought she would, telling the story of the China she knew to the Western world.

"Do you mean to say that you are going to put all that education into telling made-up stories!" her father exclaimed. "Why not do some scientific writing, something worthwhile?"

But Carie understood. Like Pearl, she knew that the work of a good novelist goes straight to a reader's heart.

"Do it, Pearl," Carie encouraged her daughter. "You are meant to be a storyteller. I have always known it."

Pearl longed to travel to parts of China she had never seen, but her mother needed her care. The days were filled with making Carie as comfortable as possible and with teaching at the new boys' school run by her father's mission board. All the young Chinese women Pearl knew·were married and raising families. The women worried over Pearl. "Why does your father not find a husband for you?" they asked. Arranged marriages were the custom in China.

Letters from America brought news of the engagements of Pearl's college friends one by one. Pearl was lonesome. She wanted to be married, too. There were very few American men in China. When she began seeing an American busi-nessman, the other missionary families objected. "You should keep company with a missionary," they said.

"But *I* am not a missionary," Pearl told them. When her father suggested a young Chinese man he knew, it was Pearl who objected. She knew the man's family would frown on his marrying an American. She began to spend time with John Lossing Buck, an American agriculturist working for the mission board.

"Lossing and I are going to be married," Pearl announced one day. Her parents went about the house in silence. They were not pleased with Pearl's decision.

"You two are behaving like Chinese parents," Pearl said angrily. "You are trying to arrange my life."

"It is not that, Pearl," Carie explained. "It is just that Lossing never reads, and we rarely see you without a book. We are afraid you will be unhappy with someone who does not understand you."

"I am going to marry him," Pearl said. The wedding took place on May 30, 1917.

Lossing and Pearl moved two hundred miles north of Chinkiang to a wheat-growing region where Lossing would be teaching American farming methods to the Chinese farmers. Pearl's friendly new neighbors invited her into their homes, to their weddings, and to other family celebrations. She soon became caught up in their lives.

Farm families, who made up 85 percent of China's population, were the real China, Pearl felt. But now there was a movement toward Westernization going on in China that upset her. Chinese graduates of Western universities were bringing their Western ideas home with them. They wanted to create what they called "The New China." Pearl was afraid that the strengths of the four-thousand-year-old culture would be lost in such a fast takeover. She longed to write about the China she knew, before it disappeared. Many days, she sat down to write. Each time, she held back. "I am too young. I have not lived enough of life to be a novelist yet," she said.

In the spring of 1921, Pearl and Lossing had a baby daughter. The nurse wrapped the unusually pretty girl in a pink blanket and handed her to her mother. "There is a special purpose for this child," she said.

They called the baby Carol, after Pearl's mother. Carie was able to enjoy her little namesake for only six months. In October, Pearl's mother died. Pearl began immediately to write the story of Carie's life. Writing down the warm memories helped ease her grief.

When the story was done, Pearl found that she

did not want to stop writing. *Now* was the time to do what she had always known she would do! She sat down and wrote "In China, Too," an essay intended for publication. The joy of seeing it printed in the *Atlantic Monthly*, an American magazine, inspired her to write a second essay.

Carie's story was put away. Someday, Pearl thought, Carol would want to read about her grandmother. Pearl had begun to worry over Carol. She was not doing the things a child over a year old should be doing. "When did your babies sit up?" Pearl asked other mothers. "When did they smile?"

"She should be talking," Pearl said anxiously when Carol had passed two and still hadn't said a word.

"All the children on my side of the family were slow developers," Lossing said. He went back to his paperwork.

"Surely something is wrong!" Pearl said when Carol was nearly four and still not talking. Carol also had trouble walking, and often her eyes were unfocused.

Lossing nodded. His wife was terribly upset. That he could see. But he did not know what to say to comfort her. Lossing did not have a way with words.

Pearl took her husband's silence for lack of

caring. She turned to her friends for support.

The Bucks had moved to Nanking, where Lossing was teaching agriculture at Nanking University. Pearl took Carol to a visiting American pediatrician there. The child was most certainly behind in her development, he said. He advised taking her to America to be evaluated by specialists.

Lossing was granted a one-year leave from his teaching. He and Pearl decided to study at Cornell University where they would be close to the doctors for Carol. Lossing, Pearl, and their silent little daughter sailed for New York. Whenever Carol slept aboard ship, Pearl found a quiet corner and wrote. Writing eased her anxiety. By the time they reached America, she had completed a story, "A Chinese Woman Speaks."

On the advice of her teacher at Cornell, Pearl sent the story to *Asia Magazine*. It could be months before she knew whether or not it sold. In the meantime, there were the doctors to see.

Pearl took Carol from doctor to doctor. The answers she received were always vague. No one seemed able to pinpoint the exact problem. "Perhaps the child is simply lacking in the company of other children," one doctor suggested. Pearl hoped that he was right. Since Pearl was unable to have any more children, she and Lossing began to think of adopting another child.

The reason for Carol's slow development was finally pinpointed by doctors at the Mayo Clinic in Rochester, Minnesota. "Your child has a fine body," one doctor said. "But mentally, she is severely retarded."

"For your sake and for hers as well," a second doctor told Pearl, "you must face the truth. The best thing you can do is find a home for the mentally retarded and leave your child there."

Pearl took Carol and walked numbly from the building. There were no homes for the retarded in China. She could not bear the thought of leaving her child here in America, thousands of miles from home.

Sadly, Pearl told her husband what the doctors had said. Would a little sister help? they wondered. It was certainly worth a try. The Bucks soon went to visit an orphanage that had been recommended to them.

The director led them to a nursery. There were a number of healthy infants. "And we have this three-month-old who refuses to eat," he said. "With good mothering, perhaps she stands a chance. Otherwise, I am afraid there is no hope."

Pearl looked down at the bald, sickly looking baby. "Give her to me," she said. When Lossing, Pearl, and Carol returned to China, tiny Janice went with them.

During the time that Pearl was visiting doctors with Carol, she had received some exciting news. *Asia Magazine* wished to buy "A Chinese Woman Speaks." The sale had lifted her spirits.

Soon after Janice's adoption, a letter from Brentano's, a New York book publisher, encouraged Pearl still further. "A Chinese Woman Speaks," the story that appeared in *Asia Magazine*, was most appealing, the publisher wrote. He suggested enlarging it to make a book. Pearl thought the story was complete as it was. Pairing it with "West Wind," a second story she was working on, would be better, she felt.

Pearl returned to China with "West Wind" scarcely begun. Day after day, she sat with a blank page of paper before her. The wastebasket filled up with false starts. The words simply would not come. Janice was eating and adjusting well to her new life, but Pearl was still too upset over Carol to think.

The weeks went by. At last she was able to send the combined stories that she called "The

Winds of Heaven" off to the publisher. When she received the publisher's reply, it was disheartening. The story in this form did not appeal to him at all, he wrote.

Sadly, Pearl put the rejected manuscript away in a drawer. She closed up her typewriter. "Whoever said you could write in the first place?" she asked herself.

Chapter Five

Pearl was pouring the breakfast coffee on a March morning in 1927 when the Chinese tailor who lived next door pounded at the door. "You must leave at once!" he cried.

Communist revolutionaries were entering Nanking. For the second time in her life, Pearl was in danger because she was a white person in a Chinese city. Pearl's sister Grace had recently come from Hunan with her husband and their small child to seek safety. With Pearl's father, who lived with Lossing and Pearl, that made eight of them to hide. Where could they go?

They heard the screech of the garden gate. The soldiers, already? Pearl peeped cautiously out the window.

It was only Mrs. Lu, their neighbor who lived over by the city wall. "Come and hide in my little house," Mrs. Lu said.

Pearl looked down at her daughters. Janice was not yet two. Six-year-old Carol would not be able to understand the situation much better than her baby sister. "Suppose the children cry?" Pearl asked.

"The revolutionaries will think they are mine and move on," Mrs. Lu said. "All children cry the same." She motioned for them to come along with her.

The eight of them spent the rest of the day and the night huddled in the little room that Mrs. Lu called home. Outside came the sounds of gunshot and the cries of an angry mob. The children did not make a sound. In the stillness of their refuge, Pearl sat thinking. This kind woman was risking her own life so that theirs might be saved. A mother reaching out to other mothers.

Why did peoples of the East and West think they were so different? Pearl wondered.

In the morning, the white families were taken to the harbor. An American ship carried them to safety in Japan. There they spent the summer. The months in the peaceful mountains of Japan restored Pearl's spirit; she found the desire to write growing strong within her again.

When the government officials said it was safe to come back to China, Pearl and her family were among the first to return. It would be necessary to spend some time in Shanghai, they were told, until clearance was given to proceed north to Nanking. Pearl loved walking through the streets of Shanghai, talking with the noodle vendors, the bakers of small loaves of bread, and all who came by. Her mind soon filled with characters and ideas for stories.

In a bookstore, Pearl discovered a worn copy of the *Writer's Guide*, printed in London. Pearl flipped through it hoping to find the names of literary agents in America. She had decided that the only way to have a book published was by sending it to an American agent, someone who would show it to different publishers there. Yes, there were two! Pearl copied down the names of the New York agents and happily went back home. On a borrowed typewriter, she went to work on a new story idea. Pearl called the novel she was beginning to shape "Wang Lung."

She promptly sent a letter to the first of the two agents she had discovered. Would he be interested in a novel about life in China? she asked. The agent's reply was disappointing. He knew of no publisher interested in Chinese subjects. Pearl decided that sending an actual story about China would prove more fruitful. She sent the second agent, David Lloyd, a letter accompanied by her "Winds of Heaven" manuscript. David Lloyd's reply was cautious. He would be glad to read the story, but in all honesty, he had never heard of a publisher interested in China.

In the summer of 1928, the Buck family returned to Nanking. The arrival was not a happy one. Their house had been used as a barrack for soldiers and then as a government hospital for cholera patients. It would be necessary to live with a Chinese family until the house could be cleaned and disinfected.

As soon as the Bucks moved back in their home, some students from the university came to see Pearl.

"We saved these books for you," they said as they handed Pearl a box. Inside was the set of blue Dickens books that Pearl had kept since her childhood. Underneath lay a manuscript, the story about Carie.

Pearl set her house in order. In the attic, she placed a very old Chinese desk she had discovered in a secondhand shop. The beauty and dignity of the desk inspired her; she longed to get back to work on "Wang Lung." Finding time to write was difficult. She was setting up housekeeping all over again, and the girls required much care. Janice often had nightmares. The sounds of gunshot and the howling mob had terrified her during that night spent at Mrs. Lu's. Carol grew more and more difficult to manage.

"If only I could find time for my writing," Pearl complained at supper one night. "I simply *must* write, or I shall die."

Lossing did not reply. He could not understand his wife's driving need to write.

Pearl said no more of the matter. At night, after the girls were in bed, she went to her desk in the attic.

Life in China was becoming increasingly dangerous for white people. Pearl worried about what would happen to Carol, a helpless child, if anything should happen to her and Lossing. The chances of having to go through more turmoil were great. It was also becoming increasingly clear that Carol needed to be in a place where trained workers could meet her special needs.

Pearl's heart went out to this daughter who would always be a child. She went about the unhappy task of writing letters to schools for the retarded in the United States. There was a school in Vineland, New Jersey, whose philosophy matched her own, she learned. Its number-one rule was that the children must be happy. Sadly, Pearl wrote the director of Vineland Training School that she wished to visit the school.

In July of 1929, Pearl, Lossing, and Carol sailed for America. Janice stayed in China with friends of the family. Lossing's survey had developed into a three-volume book. He would be working on the remainder of it at Cornell University in New York. When they arrived in America, Lossing went to Cornell and eight-year-old Carol was settled in at Vineland Training School. Pearl went on to spend some time with a friend in Buffalo, New York.

"A cablegram has come for you," her friend said one afternoon. Pearl quickly opened the official-looking envelope. "The Winds of Heaven" had been sold to John Day, a New York publishing company! The news had gone all the way to her home in China and back to New York.

Pearl was 37 now, and her dream had come true. She had become a novelist. The book would be published as *East Wind: West Wind*, a title suggested by the publisher.

Pearl's joy at the acceptance of her first novel was dampened by her sadness at leaving her daughter. When Lossing and Pearl returned to China, Pearl was deeply depressed. Her piano went untouched, her typewriter, like the much-loved musical instrument, sat unused. Friends came and went. There was nothing that could fill the emptiness.

One day, Pearl stood looking out at beautiful Purple Mountain, rising majestically beyond her attic window. It was the mountains that had restored her spirit in Japan. It was to the mountains that her mother had turned, overwhelmed with homesickness for her native land. In the stillness of the morning, Carie's words came back to her.

"You are meant to be a storyteller, Pearl. I have always known it."

Pearl turned her Chinese desk to face Purple Mountain and took out a fresh supply of paper. Now was the time to *really* write. In this spirit, she returned to "Wang Lung."

Chapter Six

The ideas for "Wang Lung" had been with Pearl for most of her life, it seemed. Now, each morning after the house was set in order and Janice was off to school, Pearl put the story down on paper.

This second novel was going to be far more than a sketch of the life of a farmer named Wang Lung. Pearl was determined to show the love and respect she felt for all the farm families of China. Wang Lung, her central character, represented all the farmers she had watched working the soil from daylight until dark. His wife O-lan grew out of all the Chinese farm women who had served Pearl suppers at tables lit by bean-oil lamps.

The north country she had gone to as a bride became her setting, and Nanking, her current home, appeared in her novel as a rich southern city. Pearl drew material from the events of her childhood as well. The servant girls she had met as a young girl at the Jewell School showed up in "Wang Lung" as Lotus and Pear Blossom. The famine that had seen Pearl and Grace filling bowls with rice on that long ago Christmas day was the basis for the great famine she wrote about.

Pearl told her story well. She had lived it.

At the end of three months, the novel was finished. She longed to discuss it with someone. But who? Her father had no heart for novels. Her visiting brother was too busy with business. The only subject Lossing was interested in reading about was agriculture. There was no one. She slipped the manuscript into an envelope and mailed it off to David Lloyd.

Almost immediately after reading the manuscript from China, David Lloyd sent it on to Richard Walsh, president of the company that published Pearl's first novel. The note he sent with the manuscript called "Wang Lung" "a remarkable piece of work." Lloyd hoped that Walsh would be as excited about this new book as he was.

Richard Walsh was very excited but not surprised. He had known that Mrs. Buck had it in her to be a great novelist, he said. It was he who had cast the deciding vote on the acceptance of *East Wind: West Wind.* "Wang Lung" was accepted immediately by the John Day Company.

The first thing Walsh did was suggest a title change. The book was published as *The Good Earth* in the spring of 1931. A week after its publication, the first edition sold out. In the next four months, forty thousand copies were sold. People did want to read about China! This news was a great boost to Pearl. Not only did she have the satisfaction of knowing that people were reading about China, but the money received from the sales of the book gave her a much-needed feeling of security.

Things were not going well in China. The Nationalists and revolutionaries were still struggling. Pearl feared that China was on the brink of war. For Janice's safety, they would soon have to leave the country.

There was a personal reason for Pearl's departure as well. The distance between her and Lossing had grown. They didn't seem able to share in each other's lives. In addition, Lossing objected to paying large amounts of money to Vineland Training School. Pearl worried that she would not have the money to keep up the expensive payments for her daughter's lifelong care. Pearl longed to be closer to her child when emergencies arose. It was time to say good-bye to China.

Pearl and Janice arrived in America in the spring of 1934. Lossing remained in China. The breakup in the Bucks' marriage could no longer be avoided. Pearl and Janice lived in an apartment in New York while Pearl started to put together a life for them in America.

If this country of her birth were to feel like home, Pearl realized, they would need a house to call their own. She wanted something old, a house that had roots. The result was Green Hills Farm, a stone farmhouse built in Pennsylvania's Bucks County in 1835. Pearl soon settled down to writing. "I've got a dozen stories buzzing around in my head," she told her publisher.

In Richard Walsh, Pearl had found a soul mate. Not since her mother, had anyone understood her so well as a writer. In 1935, Pearl and Lossing Buck were divorced. Pearl married her publisher. Soon after they were married, Richard and Pearl decided that they wanted more children. "What would you think of having some brothers and another sister?" they asked Janice. More children would be nice, Janice agreed. The three of them together went through the process of adopting two baby boys. Soon afterward, another baby boy and another baby girl were added to their family.

Pearl continued to work steadily. The years at Green Hills Farm were fruitful. With a full-time nurse to help with the children, Pearl spent many hours at her typewriter. She was working in her study in 1938 when her secretary rushed in with a startling announcement. "You've won the Nobel Prize!" she said.

The Nobel Prize was an international award given in the fields of physics, chemistry, medicine, economics, and literature and for the furtherance of world peace. The Nobel signified greatness.

"I will not believe it until we telephone Sweden and confirm it ourselves," Pearl told Richard.

It was true. Pearl had won the Nobel Prize for literature, not only for *The Good Earth*, but for all her works of literature. The many books and magazine stories she created had made her a much-loved American author.

On a gray November day, Pearl, Richard, and Richard's daughter Betty boarded the *Normandie*, a ship bound for Sweden. There Pearl would appear before the king! The idea made her nervous. What did one say to a king? she wondered.

Pearl, Richard, and Betty were ushered into an elegant hotel room. In moments, an attaché of the king arrived. He proceeded to teach Pearl how to curtsy and read her a full page of printed instructions. "Whatever else you do, do not turn your back to the king," he warned. A recent diplomat had disgraced his country by doing that very thing. Pearl was more nervous than ever. Suppose she forgot to back off the stage? Suppose she fell? America and American writers would be disgraced.

The time arrived for Pearl to mount the flag-draped platform. In front of her sat the dignified, aged King Gustav V. Pearl made her curtsy. She came face-to-face with His Majesty the King. The king looked amazingly like her father!

King Gustav leaned forward on his throne. "I have never wanted to be king," he said quietly. "I would far rather be a writer." They were friends.

Pearl got back to Green Hills Farm just in time for Christmas. Holly wreaths decorated the windows. Four little figures in red coats and leggings came running. Pearl was escorted to the door amidst a flurry of hugs and kisses.

Inside the entryway, the Chinese goddess of mercy held out welcoming arms. The fireplace sent out its warmth. The table was set with Pearl's favorite Chinese dishes. Pearl went over to the old Chinese desk and put down her briefcase. She went upstairs and hung up her coat. On the shelf above her bed stood a paper Christmas angel, made by Carol for her mother.

"And what did you like best about the trip?" Janice asked.

"Best of all was coming home," Pearl said.

Afterword

Pearl S. Buck continued to write for many years. She created well over one hundred stories that spoke out strongly against prejudice, the one thing in the world she could not stand. With the recognition and money she received from her books, she was able to make contributions to understanding between peoples of the East and West.

From 1941 to 1951, Pearl sponsored the East

and West Association. This organization sent representatives of Eastern cultures to the West and those from the West to the East. Participants were encouraged to share their lives through an exchange of foods, customs, and native arts.

Just before Christmas in 1948, Pearl received a letter from an adoption agency telling about a 15-month-old boy born to an American missionary and an East Indian. It was impossible to place the child, the letter said. Within a year, Pearl had organized Welcome House, an agency specializing in international adoption. This agency made it possible to give American homes to overseas children of mixed parentage who were in desperate need of adoptive parents.

Soon after the Korean War, Pearl was walking down a narrow Korean street when a child dressed in rags held out his hand to her for coins. Pearl looked down into the dirty face and saw a boy with bright blue eyes. Asia was full of such children, she learned, unwanted because they had Western fathers. It was for them that Pearl created the Pearl S. Buck Foundation. Contributors to the Foundation provide health care, education, and adoptive homes for children who might otherwise be beggars.

Pearl made generous contributions to the Vineland Training School, providing for research and the building of Carol Cottage, a home on the campus. As a result of such research, it is now known that children like Carol suffer from the inability of their bodies to use protein. These children can now develop normally if their diet is regulated.

Pearl S. Buck died of cancer at the age of 80. According to her wishes, she was buried beside her favorite tree on Green Hills Farm, facing east. The name on her memorial is written in Chinese.

Listed below are some of the books Pearl S. Buck wrote for children. Like her books for adults, these stories celebrate the two worlds that Pearl Buck knew.

The Big Wave. New York: The John Day Company, 1948. Illustrated with prints by Hiroshige and Hokusai.

The Chinese Story Teller. New York: The John Day Company, 1971. Illustrated by Regina Shekerjan.

Fairy Tales of the Orient. (selected, edited and introduced by Pearl S. Buck) New York: Simon & Schuster, 1965. Illustrated by Jeanyee Wong.

Matthew, Mark, Luke and John. New York: The John Day Company, 1967. Illustrated by Mamoru Funai.

My Several Worlds, abridged for younger readers. New York: The John Day Company, 1964.